I'm like no other creature

On land or in the sea.

Read on and you'll discover

Just how I came to be.

For Casey Elle,
and the unique qualities in all of us
—K. M. T. and A. S.

First published 2000 in the United States of America by
Charlesbridge Publishing
85 Main Street, Watertown, MA 02472
(617) 926-0329
www.charlesbridge.com

Originally published 1999 in Australia by
University of Queensland Press
Box 42, St. Lucia, Queensland 4067

Library of Congress Cataloging-in-Publication Data
Available upon request.
ISBN 1-57091-391-9 (reinforced for library use)
ISBN 1-57091-392-7 (softcover)

Printed in Hong Kong
(hc) 10 9 8 7 6 5 4 3 2 1
(sc) 10 9 8 7 6 5 4 3 2 1

Illustrations in this book done in ink and dye on silk
Display type and text type set in Clearface Gothic and Bodoni
Color separations by PageSet Pty. Ltd.
Printed and bound by Everbest Printing Co. Ltd.
Designed by Peter Evans

Silk-Painting Technique
Each illustration in this book has been hand drawn and painted on silk using
a combination of a latex-based ink called gutta and dyes blended like watercolor.
To fix the color, the silk is rolled up and steamed in a special machine.

Neptune's Nursery

Kim Michelle Toft and Allan Sheather

Illustrated by Kim Michelle Toft

▣ Charlesbridge

I am a wondrous creature.

My birth is so unique.

Look closely now and find me

In ocean hide-and-seek.

I'm not the playful dolphin.

She'll deliver only one.

Her family pod surrounds
    the pair

To see no harm is done.

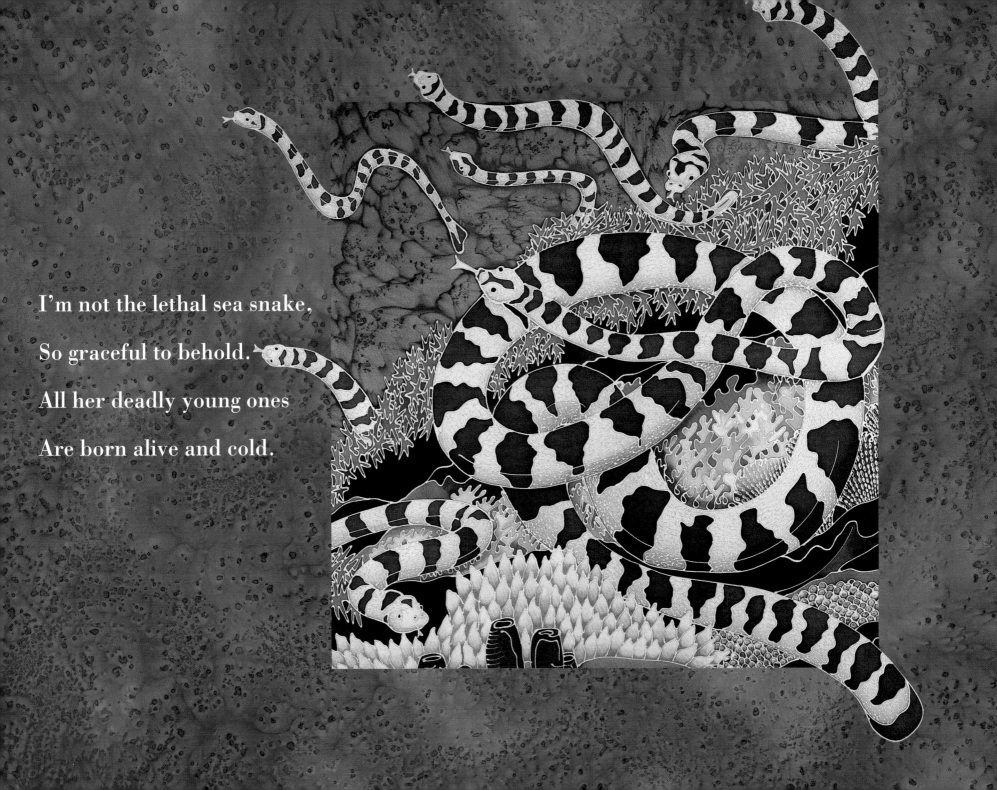

I'm not the lethal sea snake,
So graceful to behold.
All her deadly young ones
Are born alive and cold.

I am a bony creature.

Most find me hard to eat—

Except for pesky sea crabs,

Who enjoy me as a treat.

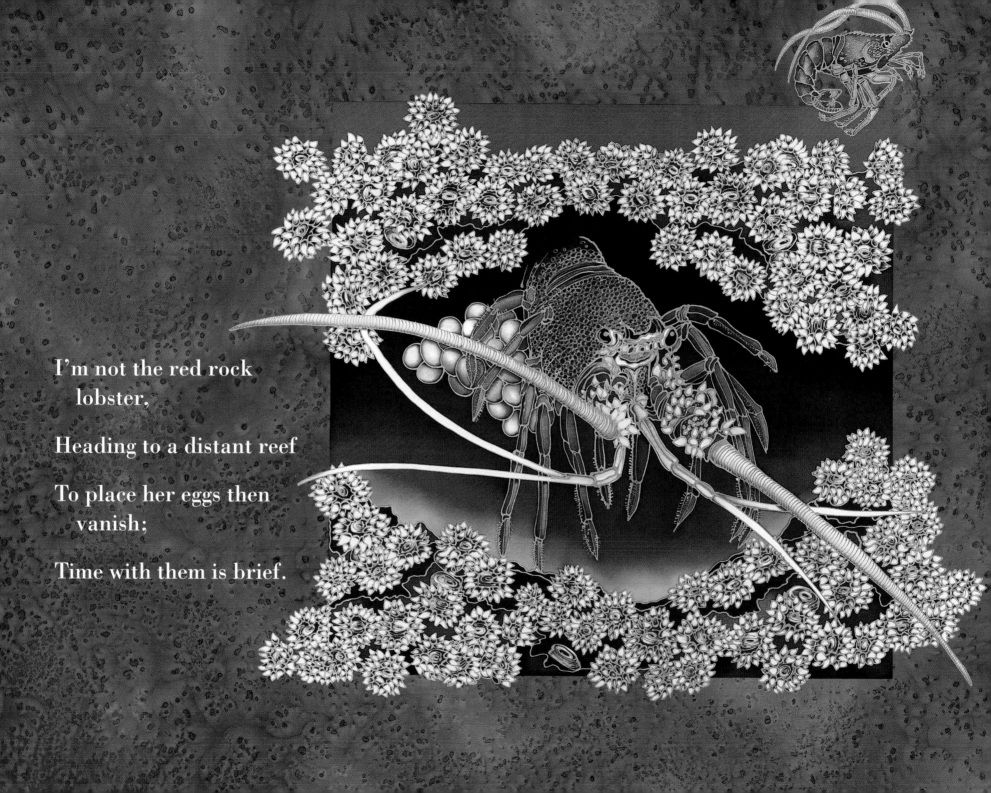

I'm not the red rock
    lobster,

Heading to a distant reef

To place her eggs then
    vanish;

Time with them is brief.

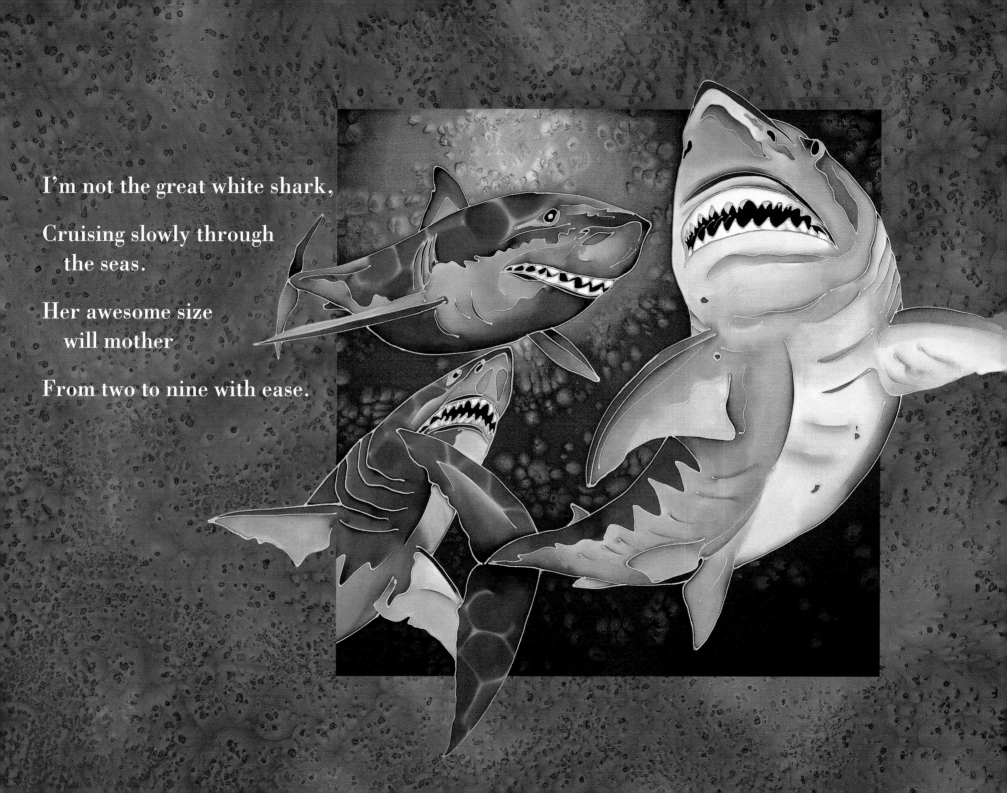

I'm not the great white shark,

Cruising slowly through
the seas.

Her awesome size
will mother

From two to nine with ease.

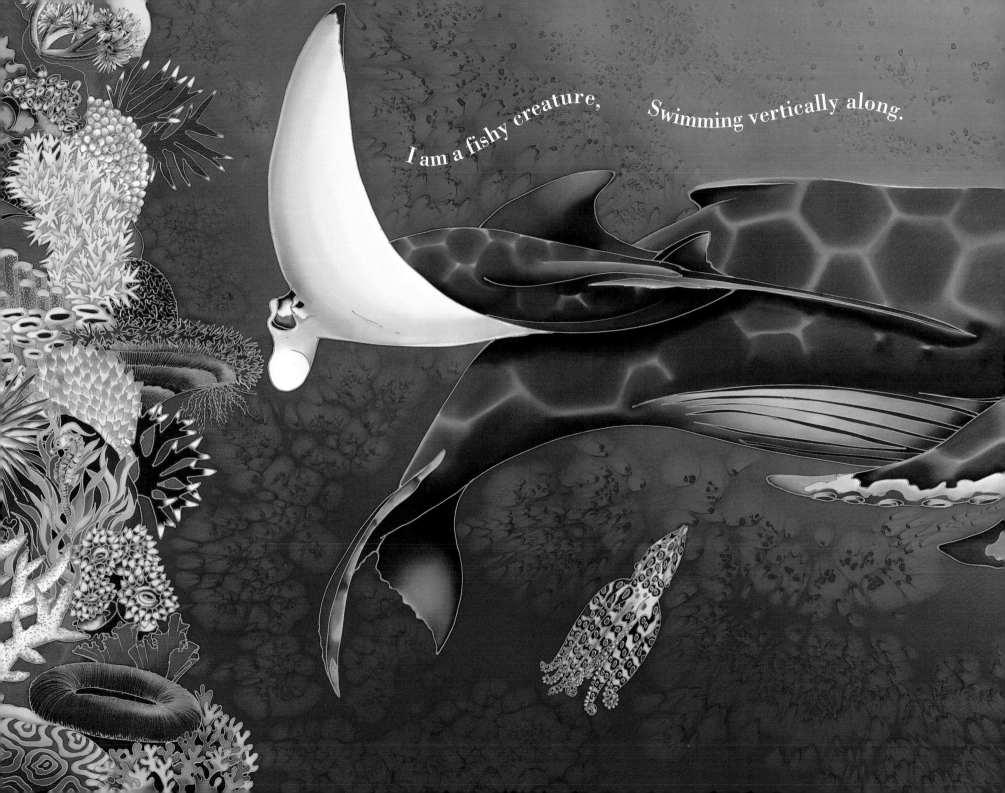

I am a fishy creature, Swimming vertically along.

My dorsal fin propels me

In a current swift and strong.

I'm not the mighty manta.

Her pup glides close below,

Protected by her wing span.

Their bond is sure to grow.

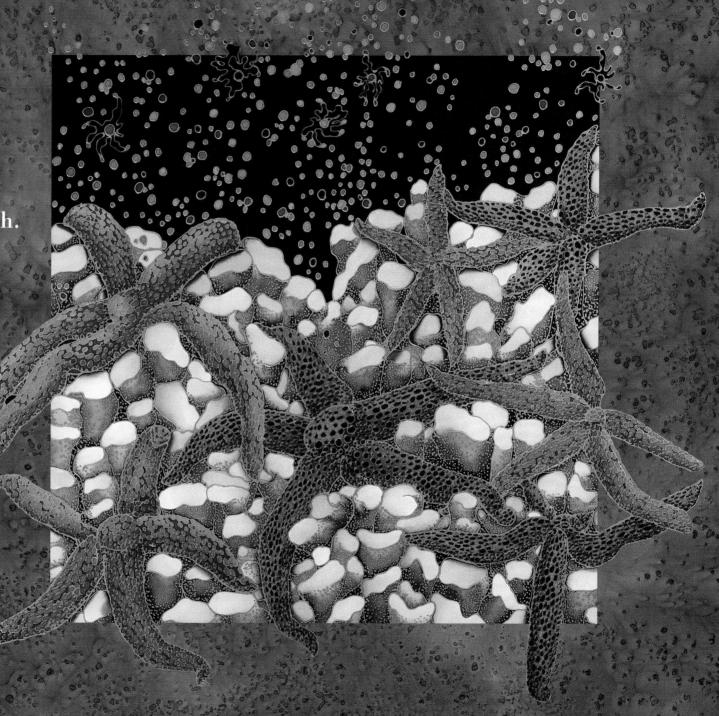

I'm not the pretty starfish.

Two million eggs she'll
    spawn,

To float and intermingle

Before the coming
    dawn.

I am a fragile creature.

My shape is quite distinct.

I'm used in ancient remedies;

I could become extinct.

I'm not the green sea turtle.

Her hatchlings have to race.

From shore to sea they
   scamper;

Many dangers they
   must face.

I'm not the blue-ringed
   octopus.

Two hundred eggs she'll lay,

Then after all have hatched,

She'll sadly pass
   away.

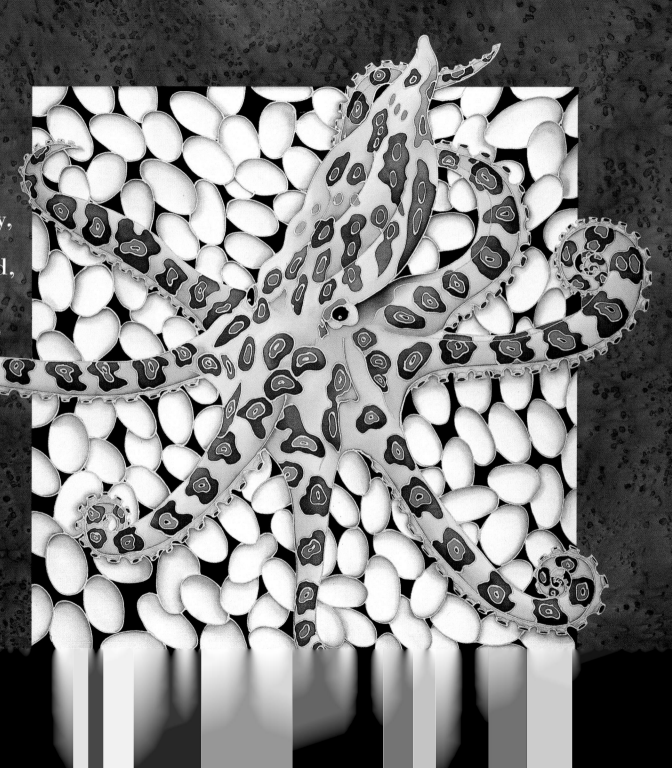

I am a hungry creature,

I am a timid creature,

Now anchored to a tree,

And when I use my camouflage,

I'm not the living nautilus

Beneath the ocean green.

Her newborn are
   a mystery—

Their birth is rarely seen.

I'm not the giant humpback.

Two calves are very rare.

Maternal instinct guides
her

Through oceans
everywhere.

Awaiting passing prey.

Both my eyes can swivel,

Each in a different way.

I'm very hard to see.

But still I haven't told you
Just how I came to be.

Unlike the other creatures

On land or in the sea,

My amazing life began when . . .

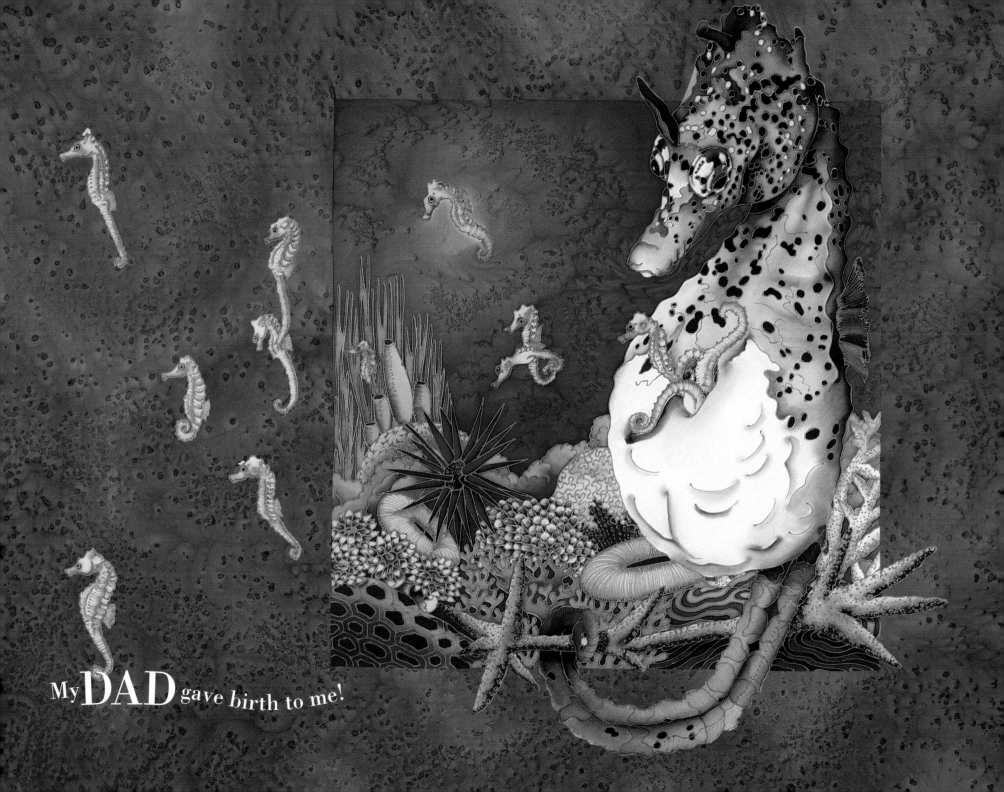

My DAD gave birth to me!

Sea Snake
reptile

There are two types of sea snakes; one (pelagic) cannot live on land at all. Although sea snakes are mainly solitary creatures, during the breeding season they gather in large numbers. The young of most species are born alive at sea, between two and twenty at a time. All sea snakes breathe air, staying underwater for up to two hours with the help of greatly enlarged lungs and special valves that cover their nostrils.

Bottle-nosed Dolphin
mammal

Like land-based mammals, the bottle-nosed dolphin is warm-blooded, breathes air, and gives birth to live young that are fed from the mother's breast. Dolphins gather in pods, or schools, "talking" to one another with a range of whistles and clicks, which are part of a simple communication system. When a pregnant female is about to give birth, she is often accompanied by other female dolphins that protect her and help her support the newborn pup to the surface for its first breath of air.

   The baby is about one meter long when born. The pup will stay close to its mother for about 14 to 19 months.

Rock Lobster
crustacean

Lobsters are decapods (they have ten legs). They have soft bodies protected by hard external skeletons. The female lays and carries hundreds of thousands of eggs underneath her abdomen, and while she does so is said to be "in berry." She eventually places the eggs under coral shelves or in caves, leaving them to hatch on their own as small larvae.

Great White Shark
cartilaginous fish

The great white shark, like the manta ray, is a fish with a cartilaginous skeleton. Because of its large size; powerful jaws; sharp, serrated teeth; and ability to swim in fast bursts, it is perhaps the best known and most feared of all sharks. Female sharks produce eggs that are fertilized internally by the male and hatch in the uterus. When ready to give birth, the female will often go to a special nursery area away from larger sharks. The mother does not stay with her newborns.

Manta Ray
cartilaginous fish

The manta ray has a cartilaginous skeleton made, not of bone, but of soft gristle or cartilage, like the end of your nose. It is one of the largest living fishes and is capable of rapid speed, sometimes leaping right out of the water and landing with a loud slap. Unlike some other rays, it does not have a stinging spine on its tail. Young are born alive, the mother giving birth to only one pup at a time, which is born wrapped in its wing flaps. Pups measure one meter across at birth. The pup stays close to its mother, swimming under her wings for protection. The average width of an adult ray is four meters.

Starfish
asteroid

A starfish is radially symmetrical, which means that its five arms spread out from a central core and exactly the same things are in each arm: respiratory, digestive, sensory, reproductive, and locomotor organs. The creature's mouth is the center of its body. The female starfish releases sex cells at the same time she releases her eggs (2.5 million per session), and these trigger the male starfish to release his sperm. As the eggs and the sperm intermingle in the sea, the eggs are fertilized.

Blue-ringed Octopus
cephalopod

The blue-ringed octopus is the smallest of all octopuses and the most deadly. It has eight tentacles and moves through the water by jet propulsion. After mating, the female lays between 100 and 200 eggs, which she keeps in a cradle she makes by turning herself almost inside out to create a dish shape. She does not feed or move for the three months it takes for the eggs to hatch. When all have hatched, she dies.

Green Turtle
reptile

Turtles are long-lived, slow-growing creatures that breathe air. The male turtle will live his life in the ocean; the female goes on land only to lay eggs. At night she will move onto a beach and scrape out a nest, into which she will lay about 125 eggs before covering it with sand and returning to the ocean. After incubating for between six and eight weeks, the eggs hatch in the sand. Moving as a group, the baby turtles dig up through the sand and burst out onto the surface in a rush before scurrying down to the ocean. They are easy prey for seabirds and carnivorous fish.

Nautilus
cephalopod

The nautilus is an ancient creature, dating back some 4,000 million years. It is very shy, living mainly in the ocean depths and rising to the surface to feed. It lives in a spiraled shell, from which the creature extends tentacles to catch its prey and to crawl on the bottom of the sea. Over a period of 50 to 60 days, the female will mate with the male and spawn eggs in very shallow places in and around coral reefs. Eggs hatch within a few months. Very little is known about the early development of the nautilus.

Humpback Whale
mammal

Whales are large marine mammals belonging to the same order as dolphins and porpoises. The humpback whale is a migratory creature, traveling thousands of kilometers each year in order to feed, mate, and breed.

The males are notable for their singing, which can be heard up to 185 kilometers away. Females (cows) normally give birth to one calf only, though twins have been recorded. There is a strong bond between mother and child.

Sea Horse
bony fish

Sea horses are small, upright fish; there are about 35 species. They live in sheltered coastal regions. Most sea horses are less than 15 centimeters long. A sea horse's body is protected by bony plates. It has a long snout, which it uses to suck its food into its toothless mouth; a prehensile tail, which it uses to anchor itself to sea vegetation; and hemispheric eyes, which stick out from its head and swivel independently of each other, allowing it to watch its prey without moving. It feeds on plankton and tiny fish and is a master of camouflage.

The sea horse, as well as some species of its close relative the pipefish, reproduces in an unusual way: the male gives birth. The female sea horse courts the male for several days. Then, during mating, she releases her eggs via a delivery tube into a special pouch in the male's abdomen. The eggs hatch in this pouch, which is lined with a spongy tissue containing a special fluid that nourishes the baby sea horses until they are born. The male is pregnant for about 40 days, during which time his stomach quickly grows to an enormous size. When the young are ready to be born, the male goes into labor, experiencing a series of shuddering contractions. Labor can last up to 24 hours, leaving the male in physical distress at the end. He gives birth to around 50 live baby sea horses, which are miniature replicas of their parents.

The sea horse's main predator is the crab, but it is increasingly under threat from humans. More than 20 million sea horses are poached annually for use in medicines. This is a lucrative trade, with sea horses selling at about $100.00 per kilo. Because of this, there is a growing fear that the sea horse will be hunted into extinction. To try to combat this threat, a project to breed sea horses in captivity has begun in Tasmania. If successful, the breeding program will encourage commercial farming of sea horses to supply the market, reducing the number of sea horses taken from the wild.

Glossary

Abdomen

The part of the body between the thorax (chest) and the pelvis (lower part of the body).

Camouflage

The means by which an animal blends into the background in order to hide itself.

Carnivorous fish

Fish that eat the flesh of other animals.

Cartilaginous fish

Fish in which the skeleton, including the skull and jaws, consists entirely of cartilage; for example, sharks and rays.

Dorsal fin

The fin on the back of a fish.

Fertilize

The action of a male sperm joining with a female egg so that the egg begins to develop.

Hemispheric eyes

Eyes that protrude (stick out) and are shaped like half a ball.

Incubate

To hatch eggs by keeping them warm, either by sitting on them (like hens) or by putting them in a warm place (like turtles leaving their eggs in warm sand).

Jet propulsion

A means of movement resulting from the discharge of a fluid or gas, usually from the rear. For example, octopuses squirt out water to make themselves move forward.

Larva

A stage in the life cycle of some animals after they hatch from eggs and before they transform into their adult shape. For example, caterpillars are the larvae of butterflies.

Locomotor

Having to do with movement.

Migratory

Roving from one region to another.

Pelagic

Living at or near the surface of the ocean.

Pod

A school or herd of whales, dolphins, porpoises, or seals.

Prehensile tail

A tail that can wrap around and grasp something. For example, American opossums' tails are prehensile. Elephants have prehensile trunks.

Respiratory

Having to do with breathing.

Sensory

Having to do with sight, hearing, touch, smell, or taste.

Skeleton

The framework of an animal's body, made of bones or cartilage.

Sperm

The male reproductive cell.

Symmetrical

A regular arrangement of parts of the body.

Tentacles

Movable, long, tubular structures that extend from the bodies of some animals, especially invertebrates (animals without backbones) such as the octopus and squid. Tentacles are often used as feelers.

Uterus

A structure inside a female animal where fertilized eggs develop. In mammals it is sometimes called the womb.

Valve

A structure that can be closed to temporarily block an opening or to keep a fluid flowing in only one direction. For example, the sea snake has a valve that stops water from entering the snake's nose when it is swimming underwater.